D1785466

NOT A PRAIRIE RIVER

BY

WALFRIED JANSEN

Best Wishes,

W. Jansen.

ILLUSTRATIONS

BY

ROBERT DOORENBOS

NOT A PRAIRIE RIVER

WALFRIED JANSEN

...and I will

trace for you our journey.
Not a prairie river
stalled on level ground,

but whitewater cutting granite...

BOREAL PUBLISHING

Copyright © 1996 Walfried Jansen

All rights reserved. No part of this publication may be reproduced, stored in a retrieval system or transmitted in any form or by any means, electronic, mechanical, photocopying, recording or otherwise, without prior written permission of the publisher, Boreal Publishing, Box 1065, Thompson, Manitoba R8N 1N9.

Canadian Cataloguing in Publication Data

    Jansen, Walfried 1949-
      Not a prairie river

Poems.
ISBN 0-9680538-0-7

    1. Canoes and canoeing—Manitoba, Northern—Poetry. 2. Rivers—Manitoba—Poetry. 3. Manitoba, Northern—Description and travel—Poetry. I.Title

PS8569.A568N68 1996 C811'.54   C96-900182-7
PR9199.3.J3778N68 1996

Illustrations: Robert Doorenbos
Printed and bound in Canada by Hignell Printing

Boreal Publishing gratefully acknowledges those who have shown support for the ideal of promoting northern writers. Our particular thanks to:

Mayor Bill Comaskey - The City of Thompson
Dale Shantz - Chicken Chef, Thompson
Jack Crolly - North River Outfitters, Thompson
Inco Limited - Manitoba Division

ACKNOWLEDGEMENTS

This book of river poems was helped along with input from Lorna Crozier at the Delta Marsh Writers Retreat, 1990, and Dennis Cooley at Sage Hill, 1992.

The poem *Where We Are* first appeared in *Other Voices*. *As The Seasons* appeared in *Quarry*. *Not A Prairie River* was originally published in chapbook format by Pachyderm Press.

The author would like to thank Robert Doorenbos for the generosity of his art work, and especially Ray and Zoe Irvine of Boreal Publishing for their vision and energy. Without their zeal this second coming would not have been possible.

NORTHERN MANITOBA RIVERS

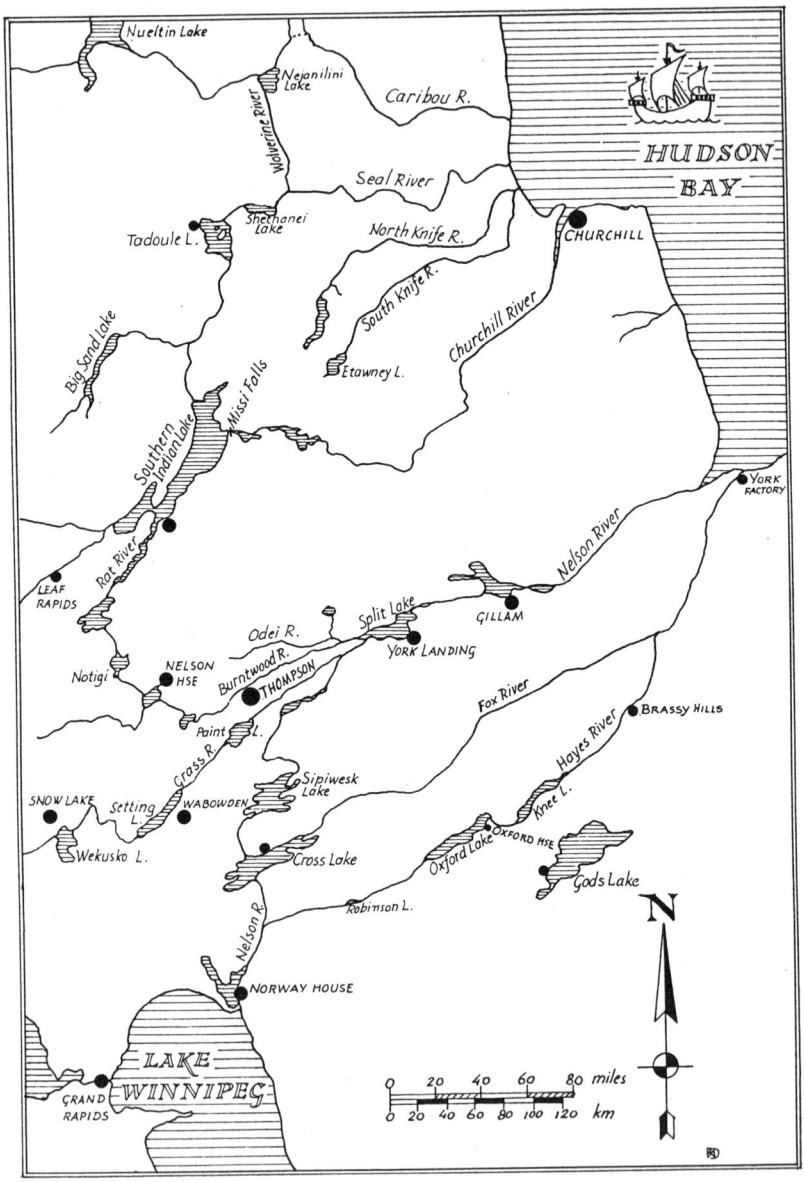

Something lost behind the ranges,
Lost and waiting for you. Go!
- - Rudyard Kipling

For Dave and the others and
the free-flowing rivers of
Northern Manitoba

CONTENTS

ILLUSTRATIONS

ROBERT DOORENBOS: Born 1928 in Alexandria, Egypt to Dutch parents and raised in Java, Indonesia. He completed his education in Rotterdam with a degree in Architectural Design. Robert has lived in Thompson, Manitoba for the past 25 years. An accomplished artist and calligrapher, he has received many awards at northern juried art shows. Since retiring from Inco he spends time between his art and assisting his wife in operating Anna's Bed and Breakfast, a hospitality business well known by international visitors to Thompson and Northern Manitoba.

PREFACE

In 1980 I was asked by some canoeing friends to join them in paddling the historic Hayes River. I had little trouble convincing my wife Ruth that this was an opportunity of a lifetime. It is not very often one gets the chance to explore the route used by the fur traders to open the western part of this great country. The Hayes River was only a 400 mile (644 kilometres) beginning to a biannual love affair with Manitoba's northern reaches. Every trip would prove to be another spiritual experience, another "opportunity of a lifetime." This is how some of the most challenging rivers, each with its own unique character, came to be re-explored. Although the north country is often hard and lonely, it possesses plenty of heart and soul and a voice loud enough to keep calling you back for more. I remember many rapids, eskers, camping and fishing spots with great fondness and longing. I do not wish to imply that these trips were filled only with sunshine and tail winds. Far from it. Those hard days on the water just added to the richness of the experience. I have borrowed accounts of Henry Kelsey, Samuel Hearne and Robert Hood to give a historical perspective to Manitoba's northern wilderness rivers.

W.J.

I AM

An escapee from Winnipeg,
I rolled north

on the wheels of an orange
Beetle. Haven't you

heard me blowing my horn?
I am Hearne,

explorer, seeker of copper,
I am Thompson, mapmaker,

come to catalogue rivers, order
tributaries by return

mail. I read whitewater, for
every rapid is a fresh

lining, every river a volume
of white words.

WINDSONG

Today's wind: a mandolin
player prying jaws,
teasing my senses. Ravens

by the river, riding
an updraft, playing tag.
I too feel the frost dam

bursting. Listen
to the water sounds
and snow settling in

on itself. Imagine
this stream of melt water
a river and I will

trace for you our journey.
Not a prairie river
stalled on level ground,

but whitewater cutting granite
on its run to the Bay.
Today the keel of my canoe

was exposed to light. Soon
the blade of my paddle
will carve new poems for you.

GULLS CALLED ME

While you were out
gulls called me.
Their crying and wheeling
I took as a sign.

Last year's lawn, brown,
dead at my feet.
The rake in my hands,
unlikely to burst

into song. Some choices
are easy. I traded for a paddle
and humped the canoe
to the river.

The air spoke of April
rawness. Ice flows and
a strip of winter on shore.
Slim green willow stalks

nodding to eddies. Still,
I needed to get on
the river, to be
whole again. Staying

close to shore I saw
kinglets and warblers,
kingfishers by the sandbank.
Coming home I heard

a whitethroat cast
his song into the air,
fishing for an ear.
There were other signposts,

some I may have missed,
and yet I longed for something
more. Maybe tomorrow
you can come too.

ODEI RIVER

The Odei River
carrying armloads
of silt, offered little
beyond a road
in and out.

> Yet Kapakaytay Falls,
> horned owls and the girth
> of spruce trees we had
> not counted on.

A broken paddle, nailed
to a tree like a crucifix,
marked the portage
around ill tempered
water.   Over the push
of this slope we sweated
with canoes, toiled
to the hum of mosquitoes.
The others, perfect
in their conviction, did not hear
the *kip, kip, kip*
crossbills in their
dip, rise, dip flight the way
they crossed the river.

They missed seeing
in the shade beside
the whisper of this trail,
a gathering of orchids;
failed to notice purple
blossoms fill me
with knowing.

AFTER KELSEY

Henry Kelsey was a poet,
now you and I know it
as a matter of fact,
but for others
(maybe even their mothers)
this may be some trivia they've lacked.

> *In sixteen hundred & ninety'th year*
> *I set forth as plainly may appear*
> *Through Gods assistance for to understand*
> *The natives language & to see their land*
> *And for my masters interest I did soon*
> *Sett from ye house ye twealth of June*

In our nineteen hundred and eightieth year
ten of us started packing our gear.
With great historical interest we soon
started from Norway House on the twenty-eighth of June.

> *Distance from hence by Judgement at ye lest*
> *from ye house six hundred miles southwest*
> *Through Rivers wch run strong with falls*
> *thirty three Carriages five lakes in all*

We stroked the Hayes at least
four hundred miles northeast
through Lower Hill Gates, around Robinson Falls,
six portages, eight lakes, small ones and all.

THE OLD SPRUCE

From behind cover
a sapling watched

Franklin go by. Self-assured
and satisfied

he now has buried time
in concentric pages.

We slept under those massive
boughs and

one by one folded
back the years.

OXFORD LAKE

always in the palm
of the river
we have been
witness   moods shifting

with the current   today
it duplicates the shore
on glass   slipping
towards the northern

edge   our canoes
slice into platinum
skin   the stitches
of our paddles

send spirals spinning
behind us   the incisions
are healing   there
will be no scars

ROBINSON PORTAGE

Between lakes
the course of the Hayes
River has multiple
fractures. Men in York
boats used iron

to skirt these breaks.
Some of the rails are still
here, half hidden in grass
and bushes. We use
our backs, count each pain

full step to the halfway
point, collapse under
the weight of our packs.
To our left we hear
water falling again

and again, alternating
green and white, washing
over rocks. We know too,
something of its coolness
and sweet taste.

ACCORDING TO HOOD

On the 9th of September, our boat was launched, rigged with one mast and a square sail. The wind was favourable, and we sailed up the stream.

On the 11th, the shallowness of the river greatly impeded us, and we were frequently obliged to get out of the boat, and lift it over the shoals. The weather was exceedingly fine, and the increased beauty of the scenery was alone a source of gratification which repaid every exertion.

On the 18th, we crossed several portages and at 2 p.m. passed a hill about 600 feet high, an object so remarkable at this level country, that the river receives its name from it. From its eminence 36 lakes can be seen.

Our astonishment at the delightful prospects of Hill (Hayes) River, was in proportion to the strength of our prejudices against the imagined barrenness and desolation of this country. It would, however, find admirers from every climate. The pine (spruce) clung to the most naked rocks, rising loftier than ever on insulated stones destitute even of moss. At the water's edge, the willow and that beautiful shrub, the American dogwood, intermingled their bright green and red leaves with their images beneath.

On the 23rd, we reached the head of Hill River, which though only 60 miles in length, had cost us nine days of unintermitting exertion.

On the 27th, we arrived at the Trout Fall Portage, having sailed 46 miles in Knee Lake. At this place, the Trout (Hayes) River falls between two rocks, about 16 feet and the portage over which the boats are dragged is very steep.

On the lst of October, we entered the Hill Gates, in which the river was confined to about ten yards between steep granite rocks, for a mile and a half. One mile is so straight that the whole perspective presents itself at once, the heights crowned with pine and larch, and the distant opening beyond by the sky; a magnificent defile which one would have thought too regular for nature, but too stupendous for art.

On the 2nd of October, we commenced our labours at the White Fall (Robinson) Portage, which exceeds half a mile in length. Mr. Franklin was traversing the banks, between two of the falls, when he slipped from the edge of a rock and rolled down a declivity 15 or 20 yards into the water. The current was not rapid, but the bank for a great extent continued too steep and slippery to afford him a firm grasp, and he was tantalized by sometimes touching the bottom, while he was, in spite of all his efforts, slowly approaching a fall. At this juncture he was descried from one of the boats, which had just been carried above the fall, and some person hastened to his relief.

BUSHED

Sixteen days on the river
and we're scratching
at the bottom
of our packs. We
crave pizzas, Big Macs,
the sweet coolness of
butterscotch ripple ice cream.
Waiting for the train
we plan, fan across
Gillam seeking succulents.

But there is nothing
here, this town
is in greater need
than we... and wait,
the sights and sounds
are strange, the walls
claustrophobic,
the odours all wrong. This is
not it
and what's more
we can't just open up
to water the bushes.
(It was damn hard
at Kettle Rapids Dam, all
that water going through.)

No way, this town
is all wrong. We'd
just as soon forget
about Big Mac
and get back on the water,
do it all again,
heading for the bush,
going back upstream.

JOURNAL ENTRIES

June 25 *1689*	*forc'd ashore by ye Ice* *now we Judged our selves to be about* *20 Leagues from Churchill River*
ye 30th *friday*	*travelled all within Land it being all hills* *& more barren then before y^e* *hills being all stones wth a coat of moss* *over y^m*
July *ye 2^d* *sunday*	*it Rained hard having no shelter but* *ye heavens for a Cannope nor no wood* *to make a fire*
ye 9th *sunday*	*Setting forward good weather* *& going as it were on a Bowling Green* *in ye Evening spyed Two Buffillo* *left our things & pursued y^m* *we Kill'd one* *they are ill shapen beast* *their Body being bigger than an ox* *leg & foot like ye same* *but not half so long a long neck & head a hog* *their Horns not growing like other Beast* *but Joyn together upon their forehead* *& so come down ye side of their head & turn* *till ye tips be Even with ye Buts* *their Hair is near a foot long*

July 6
1980
sunday

Knee Lake
in a pentamaran.
Jack boiling
soup on a camp stove
at the back
of his green scow
while we're sailing
up the thigh.

July 8
1980
tuesday

Ted filming
Dave kicking
at a large pike.
Broke water
like a fishing eagle
when he missed and snapped
his line. Called him
Fishkicker.

July 9
1980
wednesday

In modest whitewater
above Brassy Hill,
Grant and Gary wrapped
their Misty River
around a rock. Straightened
the keel, taped up
the sides. Made camp after
twelve miles.

July 10
1980
thursday

Saw a wolf on shore.
The way he looked
at us skimming
the water, two by five,
it's doubtful
he'd seen anything
like it before.

TRAVEL ITINERARY

180 miles by road
   to South Bay
10 miles by ferry
   to South Indian Lake.
60 miles by boat
   across Southern Indian Lake
   to Missi Falls.
Two days
   and 50 miles by canoe
   to Oldman River.
30 miles by float plane *
   to Etawney Lake.
Seven days
   and 200 miles by canoe
   to the coast.
   Scheduled for pick-up *
   at the goose shack
   Friday morning
   at high tide!
25 miles by boat
   across Button Bay
   to Churchill.
500 miles by rail
   to Thompson.

*Miss any of these and we're like
ducks on the water.*

THE MIGHTY CHURCHILL

carved by water
and ice; a long
blue line across
    the Shield.
Engineers choked and bled
this river from its belly,
    led the water
        astray.

Missi Falls control structure
allows a blue-green
trickle of 500 cfs
to tickle a river bed
    designed for 60,000
        floodstage.

Now this atrophied river
has wide rock
gardens where we drag
    our canoes from pool
        to pool of thin water.
From the bottom
we crane
        our necks, scan
            imposing cliffs.
Can't help but notice
the high water
mark thirty feet
    above
        us.

SOUTH KNIFE RIVER

Paddled Northern Indian
under a slow
rolling sun. Two days
oppressive with sunshine.
Could feel it
wet and heavy on our backs.
At the pick-up place trees
were stark and singular,
black from last year's fires.
Naked, we were
four paddlers on the beach,
waiting for the fire to slide
behind home plate.

In the morning
the white Cessna drew wide
circles, searching,
dropped down.   The pilot, leap
frogging over muskeg and swamp,
over eskers and creeks, put
us down nicely into
the blue bowl they call Etawney
The plane's leaving took
with it doors, walls,
telephones, the necessity
of locks.   We had
birdsong, wind touching
trees, the incredible blues
of sky and water.

Above us a jet,
like an arrowhead
on a white shaft, edged
its way to Vancouver.

On day four storm clouds
came banging
from the west, washed
away the heat with rain.
The storm left
us bucking
a northeast wind, left
us pivoting
on clouds, fog and drizzle,
on cold slanted rain.
Evenings we emerged
from our river's
tunnel, seeking
comfort in the dark
tangle of trees.

NORTH KNIFE RIVER

At the headwaters
the river talked
its way over rocks without
regret, as if knowing
its place in the scheme
of things. Now,
three days later,
there is anger
I don't wish to know.

Below the falls spires
of rock deflect water
into whirlpools. Downstream
an endless rapid
framed by sheer walls. Clouds,
low as rooftops, have been
open since noon and I
need a place to hide.

Necessity pushes flesh
beyond the tent of skin,
threads it through
a broad white line.

PALE BONES

Log cabin,
long abandoned there
on the north shore,
cold and lonely, a place
of winter's long despair.

Woodstove, covered with rust,
no one here to light a flame
Window pane, complete
reflects warm light
before cold earth can claim.

Decay has brought roof and floor
together at last,
spruce logs crumbling into dust
like pale bones of
the trapper long past.

RAIN

This morning's
rain: hesitant
drizzle. By noon
a strong vertical

current blistered
the lake. All day
rain fell, drained away
colours. All day

we paddled toward
the cold horizon.
In our slickers:
a stunning rainbow.

Now all canoes
on shore, keels
to ebbing rain.
Together with gear

we have compressed
ourselves under a tarp.
Droplets filter through
darkening spruce,

rattle overhead. An
aroma of soup
and leather boots
too near the fire.

THE ESKER

Yesterday
wind and waves,
our paddles listless
in blue-green water.
Rising trees, an esker

snake-like
in its meandering,
a gift. With a final
thrust of our paddles
the canoes rose to meet

washed sand. Beyond
the beach caribou moss,
dry and brittle, complained,
rasping as we crushed it
into footsteps. Around us

white spruce and jack pine
reached to meet the blue
of sky. We walked along
the bare spine to where
an eagle watched

with laser eye. Below
the old birch snag,
we found two feathers.
There was more, much more,
and something of you

I could not name. Swimming,
jogging, cranberries staining
our hands; the owl calling
at night. This morning
we were slow to leave

but once on the water,
paddling seemed easy. I
turned to etch the image
into memory and saw you
on wings that filled the day.

TODAY THE SUN

no roof
today   the sun
an incandescent star
an empty sky

canoes on water
angle towards
Tadoule   heat
waves distort

the ragged spruce
horizon   alongside
an esker
canoes cut clean

washed sand   running
through liquid
silver   I dive to
where the purple

cold electrifies
my body   I am
I think
laughing   a loon

WINDBOUND

Shethanei Lake
was a bitch: a tongue
of rolling water. I'm not
so sure you would
have liked it there.

A northeast clipper came
unhooked, stacked clouds,
unfurled waves
across spray decks. Muscles
unravelled while clawing
at whitecaps. The
claw marks hardly mattered
and the slow hump
of an island offered refuge.

Pinned down under
a tarp opened time
for bannock. Dave
on mandolin, Jack a kite.
I cupped a sparrow
from leeside water, warmed
him with fire.

All day wind
shredded our stories,
carried pieces
back to Tadoule. Tents,
anchored to stunted trees,
floated on moss.
Sliding into sleep
we rechristened the lake
Shit-in-the-eye.

CHANGE OF WIND

Summers are fickle
up here, blow hot
and cold with a quick
change of loyalties.

Yesterday was all wind
and rain, our spirits, blue
with cold, had rumpled into toes
of our boots. All day waves
with whitecaps slapped
the shoreline, threw sand
back at the esker,
unconcerned,
snaking off somewhere
to the northwest.

Such violence of wind
and rain reminds us
where we are
and still hope
to go, take refuge
where we find little cellars
in the weather.

Woke this morning
to find the sun
had started
without us, shooing away
night, blueing the sky.
From behind us west wind
came loping easy like
a coyote, willing
to sing to sails.

WHAT HEARNE SAID

June 23, 1770

To record in detail each day's fare fince the
the commencement of this journey, would be little
more than dull repetition of the fame ocurrences.
A fufficient idea of it may be given in a few
words, by obferving that it may juftly be faid
to have been either all feafting, or all famine:
fometimes we had too much, feldom juft enough,
frequently too little, and often not at all. It
will be only neceffary to fay that we have fafted
many times two whole days and nights; twice upwards
of three days; and once, while at She-than-nee,
near feven days, during which we tafted not a
mouthful of any thing, except a few cranberries,
water, fcraps of old leather, and burnt bones. On
thofe preffing occafions I have frequently feen the
Indians examine their wardrobe, which confifted
chiefly of fkin-clothing, and consider what part
could beft be fpared.

January 3, 1771

Many of the iflands, as well as the main land round
this Lake (Nueltin), abound with dwarf woods,
chiefly pines (spruce); but in some parts inter-
mixed with larch and fmall birch trees. The land,
like all the reft which lies to the North of Seal River,
is hilly, and full of rocks; and though none of the
hills are high, yet as few of the woods grow on their
fummits, they in general fhow their fnowy heads far
above the woods which grow in the vallies, or thofe
which are scattered about their fides.

43

April 20, 1771

*Having finished fuch wood-work as the Indians
thought would be neceffary, and having aug-
mented our ftock of dried meat and fat, the
twenty-first was appointed for moving; but one
of the women having been taken in labour, and
it being rather an extraordinary cafe, we were
detained more than two days. The instant,
however, the poor woman was delivered, which
was not until fhe had suffered all the pains
ufually felt on thofe occafions for near fifty-
two hours, the fignal was made for moving when
the poor creature took her infant on her back
and fet out with the reft of the company; and
another perfon had the humanity to haul her
fledge for her, (for one day only,) fhe was
obliged to carry a cofiderable load befide her
little charge, and was frequently obliged to
wade knee-deep in water and wet fnow. Her very
looks, exclufive of her moans, were a fufficient
proof of the great pain fhe endured, infomuch
that although fhe was a person I greatly disliked,
her diftreff at this time fo overcame my prejudice,
that I never felt more for any of her fex in my
life; indeed her fighs pierced me to the foul,
and rendered me very miferable, as it was not
in my power to relieve her.*

GHOSTS

We've been swimming
at the knee of Shethanei
cooling off
under a sun-stung
and brassy sky. Hearne
spent a sun-starved winter
here, burning piss-holes
into snow. On clear days
he may have gone
in search of ptarmigan
or caribou, hoping
to keep his neglected belly
from turning on itself.
Samuel may have heard
lake ice squeeze
off pressure ridges like
rifle shots in the night.
Perhaps he spent evenings listing
the countless forms of violence
of snow and wind. I don't know,
can only imagine his wanderings
and musings. That winter is long
gone and his footsteps have melted
with the snow, been washed
off the esker by rain.

Groping for last year's
cranberries we found
shallow graves cut
into moss and sand.

Archaeologists have been here,
painfully brushing
against this sacred ground.
They have taken all
the bits and pieces
Hearne left behind.
Now ghosts of that winter drift
aimlessly, have nothing
to come back to.

PADDLESTROKES

In need of healing
Paddlestrokes have taken me
to wild water to blast
the soul clean.

Wee-sa-kay-jac sent
Ma-heegun the wolf
and Ma-Kwa the bear.
Mang, the loon,
uncoiled silver notes
so clear we knew
we were alone.

When rivers buckled
into rapids I felt
the pulsing earth, heard
Mishipizhiw rumble in anger.

I drank the water, now
wild rivers flow in me.
The thirst I carried is gone,
lost in Deaf Rapids. But
like water flowing in any river,
more will follow,
carrying in its hip
pocket a louder,
more desperate call.

Memories, like pond water,
lose clarity in time.

Always one more river,
one more rapid to run.

GROUNDED

Raindrops f
         a
         l
         l from ruptured

              h   t   e
clouds,   s   a   t   r   on

        the dull red roof
of my van.   small droplets
              p, greet whole
     bounce   u

 drops coming d
              o
              w
              n. We've spent
         two days
 w   a   i   t   i   n g;
    can't fly in the rain.
   Ravens too, have hunkered
into patience. Two rivers on my street.
  Canoes need water to float,

         high ceiling
 we need a   to fly.

  The sun, tomorrow the sun.

TUNDRA MADNESS

Portaging canoes we are
a dotted line between
two rivers; the horizon,
a thin wafer beyond
the water. The tundra does

not breathe and the only
sound, a whimbrel,
its cry at our intrusion.
Briefly I imagine us alone.
Tramping through moss

soaked in old water we
stir a black storm of flies.
We cough and hack, try returning
to life those drawn
in through laboured breathing.

Chainsaws desperate
in our ears. They seek my softest
skin: leave a small fever
for others. Our thoughts are caged
while muscles burn.

I swear these pests are
demon-bred and when I get
home, I'll tell you a story
about six wendigos
in the barrenlands.

ARCTIC SUMMERS

Arctic summers

arthritic,

advance slowly

over muskeg,

permafrost.

Tread painfully

across the treeline.

Hesitate behind

each tree. The

tundra runs

a marathon

stopping

only for

ice.

TODAY HAS BEEN ENDLESS

The Caribou is a dream
of sweet water. Elevation drops
four feet per mile, pulling water
into a long white race.
We're chasing a river,
it keeps running away.
Today has been endless
whitewater and in every rapid
my fear has pushed up boulders.
Wired to nuclear core, the eyebeam
navigates, lasers the paddle,
its pull and pry. Overload
can burn the carbon fuse.

This day is done, the sun
slides into the unknown.
We have fire and bannock
spiced with cranberries. The others
joke, laugh, talk
of rapids run. I listen
to a robin spilling itself
onto the extreme edge
of day as it melts, blood
seeping into the blackening
cradle of spruce.

I think of you
at home watching
a movie with the girls
or reading
Wilderness Tips,
perhaps sleeping,
encased in dreams.
I must tell you, today
I discovered
strange and noisy wings.

CARIBOU RIVER

This bed is a collection
of rain and snow, a
gathering of dreams. From
a distance we hear
the anger, head for shore.
Walking the white pain
of broken river, reading
the water for passage.

Our minds locked
on focus we start
an upstream ferry, allow
current to swing
the bow towards pitching hay
stacks. Staying left
of the keeper,
colliding with water, down and
up and down through white curls.
Leaning hard, knees braced
to pry... pry... prry
our way right of a boulder,
follow the vees. Slicing
through foam I taste
cool spray touched
by the sun.

Downstream the river, folding
on itself, has swallowed
the dream, shattered my image
against rocks. The canoe
jammed against boulders
and I, one foot under
the seat, a soft mass
suspended in rapids. Exploding
to surface, paddle in hand
knuckles white as the water.

THE CROSSING

from the wind
whipped ridge   caribou
trails   winding between

boulders   converged
in the willows
at the crossing   rapids

sheltered the purple
greyling   alone
by the river

at sunset   i tossed
my lure   entered
a scarlet womb

I AM WOLF

Wakened by amber
I watch the sky lift, the sun
a balloon on fire.
Beyond the beating

of a heart I think is mine
the tundra holds no sound.
Flowers play their silent
symphony of colours.

I am wolf and you
white wolf beside me
watching sun devour night.
This garden where

my solitude grows; the rise
and fall of the loon's cry.
Here the sky is still
large, unmarked, unbroken.

Seasons follow seasons still
there is no aging only
an imperceptible deepening
of caribou trails.

YOU & I

I've paddled
the length of this river,
tracked its moods
from white
caps to calm,
to current with gravel
in its throat.

Right now,
by tamarack
and boulders on lap
of sparse shore,
I watch
the river lean
clear blue glass
downhill.

We are like this
river when
our soft easy words
slide toward
a white rage.

WHERE WE ARE

Someone has been here
        before us, has
put twin shores
            on paper. Each
day we study
            the map
    for a God's eye view
where we are, where
    we hope
        to peg down
            night.

For you and I, the
            oak and the willow,
        heron and
                swallow,
    our course is
            uncharted. The end
    is somewhere
            beyond the dark
        restrictions of now.   Before
    we get there, we will
        need to gather
    up rain, head
                winds, current
        and the lake's blue
                mirror.
    At times we will have
            to stop
        and put down
                names.

61

NO BULLET TRAIN

No bullet train
from Churchill to speed
my way home. Only
this slow worm,
winding rails that stretch
and stretch their inches
across empty tundra miles.

My body knotted
into stiff seats. Spasms
of my back echo
whining springs: a
night of bruised sleep. I
curse the long hours,
this tired train.

I know you will be there
in the morning but
for now this train
has me longing for eskers,
where sleep came easy
on moss and the rush
of a distant rapid was
Eine Kleine Nachtmuzik.

I REMEMBER

1. the raft
    of forty-five
    l⁄ons on Knee Lake
    the generosity of wind.
    That night, under cover
    of storm, the scheming wind
    did an about face,
    tried its damnedest
    to push us back
    in the morning.

2. the mink
    on the island carrying
    its young
    between white needles.
    Later, another,
    so cancerous with fear,
    went over a falls
    just to get
    away. That evening
    the smoked sun slipped behind
    a veil, buried
    itself and rose again
    to flood
    the shores of Nippon.

3. the otter
   at the head
   waters
   drawing its catch
   on shore.
   It was about here
   the Knife slipped
   into my heart.

4. the lynx
   coming to the river
   to accept
   its charity of geese.
   At such times
   birdsong dies
   in stifled throat
   heartbeat
   stains the earth.

5. two seals,
   sleeping on a rock,
   torpedoed up river
   when we shot
   the rapids.
   At the bottom
   we stopped,
   watched the river
   stand up and dance.

6. the wolf
   swimming circles around
   the rooted caribou
   on a sandbar.
   Wolf was reluctant
   to leave, caribou
   refused. The river
   chose not to notice,
   carried us
   right on by.

7. These
   are the creatures
   we caught
   in unstoppered sunlight.
   The others silent
   tangled in
   dark green shadows,
   kept their flowering
   traumas hidden.

AS THE SEASON'S

As the season's
last leaves linger
beyond September,
people, healed by
summer, retreat to mazes.

The lakes, no longer
loon-laughing, grow
restless, throw whitecaps
at the shore. Shorelines
wear them leaf-naked
and without bird-voices, wait
for silent snow. Soon ice,
like eyelids will calm
the water into
a long cold sleep.

And I'll put away
my paddle: use winter
to pass the time
until spring.

NOTES ON THE TEXT

Henry Kelsey   Taken from *Hommage, Henry Kelsey* by Jon Whyte.
a/long prairie lines, Daniel S. Lenoski Ed. Turnstone Press 1989.

Samuel Hearne   Taken from *A Journey From Prince Of Wales's Fort In Hudson's Bay To The Northern Ocean* by Samuel Hearne. M.G. Hurtig Ltd., 1971.

Robert Hood   Taken from *To The Arctic by Canoe, 1819-21* by Robert Hood. C. Stuart Houston Ed. McGill - Queen's University Press, 1974.

Kapakaytay Falls   At approximately 70 feet (21.3 metres) it is Manitoba's highest waterfall.

Deaf Rapids   A particularly violent stretch of water at the mouth of the Seal River. When approaching these rapids, no sound can be heard from them.

Wee-sa-kay-jac   A supernatural Indian who is regarded as a trickster and creator in Cree legends.

Mishipizhiw   A cat-like demi-god that rules the water.